Animal Adaptations

Flight

PAMELA McDOWELL

www.av2books.com

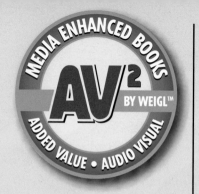

AV² provides enriched content that supplements and complements this book. Weigl's AV² books strive to create inspired learning and engage young minds in a total learning experience.

Your AV² Media Enhanced books come alive with...

 Audio
Listen to sections of the book read aloud.

 Key Words
Study vocabulary, and complete a matching word activity.

 Video
Watch informative video clips.

 Quizzes
Test your knowledge.

 Embedded Weblinks
Gain additional information for research.

 Slide Show
View images and captions, and prepare a presentation.

 Try This!
Complete activities and hands-on experiments.

... and much, much more!

Go to **www.av2books.com**, and enter this book's unique code.

BOOK CODE

T963792

AV² by Weigl brings you media enhanced books that support active learning.

Published by AV² by Weigl
350 5ᵗʰ Avenue, 59ᵗʰ Floor
New York, NY 10118
Website: www.av2books.com

Library of Congress Cataloging-in-Publication Data
McDowell, Pamela, author.
Flight / Pamela McDowell.
    pages cm. -- (Animal adaptations)
ISBN 978-1-4896-3671-3 (hard cover : alk. paper) -- ISBN 978-1-4896-3672-0 (soft cover : alk. paper) -- ISBN 978-1-4896-3673-7 (single user ebook) -- ISBN 978-1-4896-3674-4 (multi-user ebook)
1. Animal flight--Juvenile literature. 2. Wings (Anatomy)--Juvenile literature. 3. Adaptation (Biology)--Juvenile literature. I. Title. II. Series: Animal adaptations (AV2 by Weigl)
QP310.F5M33 2016
591.5'7--dc23

                    2015000830

Printed in the United States of America in Brainerd, Minnesota
1 2 3 4 5 6 7 8 9 19 18 17 16 15

052015
WEP051515

Project Coordinator Aaron Carr
Art Director Terry Paulhus

Every reasonable effort has been made to trace ownership and to obtain permission to reprint copyright material. The publishers would be pleased to have any errors or omissions brought to their attention so that they may be corrected in subsequent printings.

Photo Credits
Weigl acknowledges Getty Images as its primary photo supplier for this title.

Contents

AV² Book Code.................................. 2

What Is an Adaptation?................... 4

What Is Flight?................................... 6

How Do Animals
Use Flight?... 8

Types of Flight 10

How Does It Work?......................... 12

Timeline 14

How Humans Use Flight 16

Flight and Biodiversity................... 18

Conservation 20

Activity 21

Quiz 22

Key Words/Index............................ 23

Log on to www.av2books.com 24

What Is an Adaptation?

Animals have unique features that help them survive. These features are called adaptations. Adaptations develop slowly, over thousands, or even millions, of years. An adaptation begins with a change that helps an animal survive. If the change is successful, it passes on down through the **generations**.

Adaptations are usually influenced by the animal's environment. Some animals live in places that are very hot, cold, wet, or dry. Some animals live where there are many **predators**. Some animals live where there is very little food. Animals must adapt to survive in these challenging environments. Adaptations will make the **species** stronger.

Flight is a type of adaptation. Animals use it to escape danger, find food, catch prey, and find a mate. Flight allows an animal to live in more than one place. For example, many types of birds **migrate** to a warmer climate each fall. This ability to change **habitat** is also an advantage to animals in other ways. It means they can move easily if their natural environment can no longer provide the food and shelter they need.

Flight lets animals find prey over a large area. A kestrel can see tiny animals from 65 feet (20 meters) up in the air.

4

AMAZING FLIGHT ADAPTATIONS

Peregrine Falcon

The peregrine falcon is the fastest bird. It can fly about 100 miles (160 km) an hour and can dive at 200 miles (320 km) an hour.

Monarch Butterfly

The monarch butterfly is a strong flier. When migrating, it can fly more than 2,000 miles (3,200 kilometers).

Squid

Some squid can launch themselves into the air with a blast of water from their bodies. They then spread their tentacles and fins to form wings. They can stay in the air for about 3 seconds and travel about 100 feet (30 m).

Bat

Bats are the only mammals with wings. They clean their wings carefully every day.

What Is Flight?

Four groups of animals developed adaptations for flight millions of years ago. One group was the pterosaurs. These flying reptiles have been **extinct** for millions of years. The other three groups are insects, birds, and bats. Although these animals are not related to one another, they adapted flight in similar ways.

Animal adaptations for flight focus on the four forces of flight. These include weight, or **gravity**, lift, drag, and thrust. An animal or airplane in flight is in the middle of a tug-of-war among the four forces. In order to take off, lift must be greater than weight, and thrust must be greater than drag.

FORCES OF FLIGHT

Lift
Because of the shape of the wings, the air travels faster above the wings than below them. The air pressure builds up under the wings because the air is traveling more slowly. That pressure pushes the wings up, creating lift.

Thrust
This force propels the animal forward. An animal creates thrust by flapping its wings. Thrust depends on the strength of an animal's flight muscles and how fast it can flap.

Drag
When an animal is flying, the air pushes against it. This is called drag. It slows the animal down. Drag pulls in the opposite direction to thrust.

Weight
Weight is the effect of the force of gravity on the flying animal. Gravity pulls objects toward Earth.

BIRD ADAPTATIONS FOR FLIGHT

The heavier a bird is, the more its other features must adapt to allow it to fly. The larger a wing is, the greater the lift it produces. Therefore, birds with small wings need to flap their wings faster to get the same lift as birds with large wings.

GREAT BUSTARD

The great bustard is one of the heaviest flying birds. Males can weigh up to 35 pounds (16 kilograms). These birds need a wide **wingspan** of about 100 inches (250 centimeters) to stay in the air. Great bustards fly with slow, regular beats of their powerful wings.

BEE HUMMINGBIRD

The bee hummingbird is the smallest bird in the world. It weighs about 0.07 ounces (1.9 grams), which is less than a penny. It has a wingspan of 1.3 inches (3.3 cm). It beats its wings 80 times a second. The bee hummingbird's flight muscles make up about one-third of its body weight.

How Do Animals Use Flight?

Many animals use flight as their main way of moving around. Flying may seem effortless and fun, but it can be tricky. Some animals must warm their bodies before flying. A bee warms its flight muscles and wings by vibrating its wings. Landing may use less energy than flying, but it requires more skill. Excellent judgement and coordination are needed to land on a tree branch. Even landing on water can be difficult. A swan uses its feet as brakes, but landing can be difficult if the water is rough. Practice and adaptation are needed for perfect flight.

Brown pelicans have a streamlined body and waterproof wings. They dive into the ocean at high speeds to catch fish.

Flight in a Food Pyramid

Flight can play an important role for many animals in a **food pyramid**. Flying **tertiary consumers**, such as eagles, hawks, and ospreys, can soar without flapping their wings as they study the land or water for prey. These birds can then fold their wings and dive at great speed to catch their prey. Flying **secondary consumers**, including bats and birds such as bee-eaters, catch insects in the air. Flying **primary consumers**, such as bees and small birds, use flight to escape predators. They also use flight to move easily from plant to plant.

Tertiary Consumer
The black kite is a type of hawk. This large **carnivore** eats small animals to gain the energy it needs to survive.

Secondary Consumers
European bee-eaters are secondary consumers. These birds will catch and eat almost any flying insect, including bees, dragonflies, and butterflies.

Primary Consumers
Bees are primary consumers. They get their energy by feeding on nectar and **pollen** from plants. They also sometimes eat resin, a sticky fluid produced by some types of trees.

Producers
Producers are plants. They take in energy from the Sun. When animals eat producers, this energy passes to the next level of the pyramid. In this way, producers support the entire food pyramid.

Types of Flight

There are two types of flight in animals. Active flight is also called "true flight" or "powered flight." Animals that have adapted active flight have wings they can flap to create lift. They use their own energy to rise into the air from land, water, or trees.

Many other animals have adaptations for "passive flight." Some species of frogs, squirrels, lizards, spiders, and snakes glide using loose flaps of skin or other adaptations. These animals cannot direct their flight well. They cannot create lift. They live in and around trees, and use flight only when necessary.

It takes a great deal of energy for a swan to lift its heavy body into the air. Swans then save energy by flying in a V formation.

AMAZING TYPES OF FLIGHT

Parachuting

Large **membranes** and loose skin flaps can be used to catch air, just like a parachute. The Wallace's flying frog is one of the largest tree frogs to adapt flight. Being able to fly is an advantage when it is hunting for prey.

Active Flight

All animals capable of active flight have wings, but only birds have feathers. Feathers are light and **flexible**, but very strong. Tail feathers help birds to steer. They also act as a brake. Many birds can control their feathers and the shape of their wings.

Gliding

An animal must launch from someplace high in order to glide. Colugos have adapted flight more successfully than any other mammal, except bats. A membrane that stretches from a colugo's face to its tail acts like a sail.

Ballooning

Some species of spiders weave silk into balloons that are so light they can be carried in the wind. Ballooning helps young spiders leave the nest.

How Does It Work?

It has taken thousands of years for birds, bats, and insects to adapt active flight. Wings are their most obvious adaptation. The shape and angle of the animal's wings determine how much lift it can create. Air moves more quickly over the top surface of a large curved wing than under it. It is the difference in air movement that creates the difference in air pressure, and air pressure is what creates lift for the animal.

Animals that fly have become lighter over time. An insect's hard outer shell is its skeleton. This kind of skeleton is strong and lightweight. Birds have adapted their skeletons to be lightweight as well. They have fewer bones than mammals. Their bones and feathers are hollow and light but very strong. Beaks are also lighter than heavy jaw bones and teeth. Many birds have adapted a large, strong **sternum** to support the flight muscles. The area of a bird's brain that controls its muscles is very well developed.

A golden eagle has a wingspan of 6 to 7.5 feet (1.8 to 2.3 m). It can swoop on its prey at 150 miles (240 km) an hour.

WAYS ANIMALS USE ACTIVE FLIGHT

Soaring

Large birds often use warm air currents rising up from the ground to give them added lift. This is called soaring. Soaring allows a **raptor** to travel long distances using very little energy as it looks for food on the ground.

Hovering

Hovering is staying in one place in the air. Bees hover when they gather pollen from flowers. A bee's wings can move forward, backward, up, and down. The wings flap more than 100 times in one second.

Gliding

Animals that have adapted passive flight can only glide from a high place to a lower place, but animals that have adapted active flight can create lift, change direction, and change speed while gliding. They do this by changing the angle of their wings. Birds and some bats can glide in this way.

Flapping

A bird moves its wings up and down. A bat uses the strong muscles in its back and chest to move its wings in a rowing motion.

Timeline

An adaptation for flight helps members of a species adapt to changing environments. They can be flexible, changing their **habitat** when necessary. This flexibility helps a species to survive.

Owls have adapted well to very different habitats. They live in all parts of the world except Antarctica. Owls live in grasslands and in deserts. They live on plains and in forests. They live in rain forests and in cities.

Silent flight has helped owls to survive for millions of years. An owl can hear the slightest noise made by its prey, but prey cannot hear an owl coming.

OWL ADAPTATIONS

65 million years ago

The first owls appear. They exist at the same time as pterosaurs.

50 million years ago

The owl population is strong. There are now at least four **families** of owls, with many species. Some owls are about twice the size of today's barn owls. One type of owl cannot fly.

20 million years ago

There are now only two families of owls. One has existed for millions of years, and includes barn owls. These owls live in Europe. The other family is quite new, includes great gray owls, and lives in Europe and North America. Now, all owls can fly.

10 million years ago

Owls have specialized feathers for silent flight. Some feathers have jagged edges to muffle the sound of air flowing over the wings. Some are velvety, to absorb sound.

Today

There are 180 species of owls. One of the largest owls is the Eurasian eagle owl, which weighs between 3 and 9 pounds (1.3 and 4 kg). The smallest is the sparrow-sized elf owl, which weighs 1 to 1.5 ounces (28 to 42 grams).

How Humans Use Flight

Since ancient times, people have studied birds in flight and tried to build machines that would fly. However, it was not until just over 200 years ago that the first successful powered aircraft were built. Since then, human understanding of flight has developed quickly. Today, flight is used for transportation, defense, search and rescue, space exploration, and many other activities.

Researchers have found bees at heights of 30,000 feet (9,000 m). That is the height of Mount Everest, the world's tallest mountain. Helicopters struggle to hover at that height because the air is too thin to give them the lift they need. Studies found that the bees changed the beat pattern and angle of their wings to fly in the thin air. Scientists are using what they have learned about bee flight to adapt helicopters in the same way.

Airplanes have made a huge difference to the way people travel. Instead of spending weeks on a ship, people can get to the other side of the world in just under a day.

Humans have studied dragonfly and hummingbird flight to create unmanned aerial vehicles (UAVs). UAVs are sometimes called drones. They are used in the military, search and rescue operations, photography, and farming.

Scientists are studying how hawk moths control their flight in high winds. They are hoping the information will help them to make UAVs more stable.

Flight and Biodiversity

Biodiversity is the variety of animals and plants within an area. Each plant and animal species in an **ecosystem** plays a role in the food pyramid. Species depend on each other for survival. A greater variety of species in an ecosystem will create balance and encourage **natural selection**.

Flight is important to biodiversity. Bees and other insects rely on flight to move from flower to flower, gathering pollen. When they do this, they are helping plants reproduce. Plants also depend on bats and birds to control the insect population. Insect pests could destroy crops and forests if not controlled.

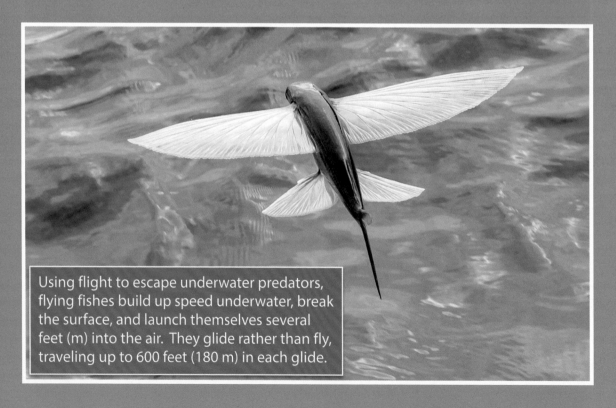

Using flight to escape underwater predators, flying fishes build up speed underwater, break the surface, and launch themselves several feet (m) into the air. They glide rather than fly, traveling up to 600 feet (180 m) in each glide.

The ability to fly has helped birds survive for 150 million years. Today, there are about 8,000 species of birds. Each species has adaptations for survival in different environments. Birds help keep ecosystems in balance by eating insects and small rodents, pollinating flowers, and spreading seeds from fruit.

A hummingbird moves its wings in a figure eight pattern in order to hover while sipping nectar from a flower.

A dragonfly has two pairs of wings, controlled separately. Having four wings helps it to gain speed very quickly.

Conservation

Conservationists study the loss of biodiversity. They also try to prevent further loss of habitats and species. Loss of natural ecosystems, such as rain forests, upsets the balance of biodiversity. Colugos, flying frogs, and flying squirrels depend on trees for flight. Without a high place to jump from, their adaptations for flight are useless. In the same way, the destruction of wetlands can change the migration and nesting patterns of birds that rely on these areas.

Biodiversity is often lost because of human activities, such as logging, pollution, and farming. Groups such as the World Wildlife Fund work to protect animals and natural environments. Other conservation groups, including Ducks Unlimited and Bat Conservation International, focus on specific species.

By putting a band on a bird's leg, wildlife workers can follow the bird's movements. Banding helps them get such information as when the bird migrates and where it goes.

Activity

Match each animal with the type of flight it has developed.

1 Squid

2 Spider

3 Owl

4 Wallace's flying frog

A Parachutes, using large membranes and loose skin to catch the air

B Balloons, using wind to carry it away

C Flies silently, surprising its prey

D Jumps out of the water to escape predators

Answers: 1. D 2. B 3. C 4. A

Quiz

Complete this quiz to test your knowledge of flight.

1 How is flight useful for flying fishes?

A. They can escape predators in the water

2 What was the group of flying reptiles called?

A. Pterosaurs

3 What are the four forces of flight?

A. Weight, lift, drag, and thrust

4 Why do swans fly in a V formation?

A. It saves energy

5 How are the bones of birds and mammals different?

A. Birds have hollow bones

6 What animals have scientists studied when creating drone technology?

A. Dragonflies, hummingbirds, and hawk moths

7 How do flowers benefit from the flight adaptation of bees?

A. Bees help plants reproduce by distributing pollen

8 Why are trees important for colugos and other animals that use passive flight?

A. They provide a high place from which to launch

9 What are two adaptations that help an owl fly silently?

A. Some feathers have jagged edges and some are velvety to absorb sound

10 How is active flight different from passive flight?

A. Active flight requires flapping to create lift; passive flight requires launching from a high perch and gliding

Key Words

carnivore: meat eater

ecosystem: all the living things that exist in a particular habitat

extinct: no longer living anywhere on Earth

families: classification relating to groups of related plants or animals; a family is bigger than a species

flexible: able to bend easily without breaking; able to change

food pyramid: a pyramid-shaped diagram of a food chain, with producers at the bottom and tertiary consumers at the top

generations: relating to the normal life spans of animals

gravity: the force that pulls objects toward the center of Earth

habitat: the natural environment of a living thing

membranes: very thin layers of tissue or skin

migrate: move from one area to another at a particular time of year

natural selection: a process whereby animals that have better adapted to their environment survive and pass on those adaptations to their young

pollen: very fine powder produced by flowers, which fertilizes seeds and is transported by wind and animals

predators: animals that hunt other animals for food

primary consumers: animals that feed on plants

raptor: a meat-eating bird, such as a hawk

secondary consumers: animals that feed on plant-eating animals

species: a group of plants or animals that are alike in many ways

sternum: the bone located in the center of the chest

tertiary consumers: animals that feed on other animals

wingspan: the distance from the tip of one wing to the tip of the other wing in a bird or an airplane

Index

airplanes 6, 16

Bat Conservation International 20
bats 5, 6, 9, 11, 12, 13, 18, 20
beaks 12
bee-eaters 9
bees 8, 9, 13, 16, 18, 22
birds 4, 5, 6, 7, 9, 11, 12, 13, 16, 18, 19, 20, 22
bones 12, 22
bustards 7
butterflies 5, 9

colugos 11, 20, 22

drag 6, 22
dragonflies 9, 17, 19, 22
drones 17, 22
Ducks Unlimited 20

eagles 9, 12

falcon 5
feathers 11, 12, 15, 22
fishes 8, 18, 22

flight, active 10, 11, 12, 13, 22
flight, passive 10, 13, 22
frogs 10, 11, 20, 21

generations 4
gravity 6

hawks 9
helicopter 16
hummingbird 7, 17, 19, 22

insects 6, 9, 12, 18, 19

kestrel 4
kite 9

lift 6, 7, 10, 12, 13, 16, 22
lizards 10

membranes 11, 21
moths 17, 22

ospreys 9
owls 14, 15, 21, 22

pelicans 8
predators 4, 9, 18, 21, 22

prey 4, 9, 11, 12, 14, 21
pterosaurs 6, 15, 22

rodents 19

snakes 10
spiders 10, 11, 21
squid 5, 21
squirrels 10, 20
sternum 12
swans 8, 10, 22

teeth 12
thrust 6, 22

unmanned aerial vehicles (UAVs) 17

weight 6, 7, 22
wings 5, 6, 7, 8, 9, 10, 11, 12, 13, 15, 16, 19
wingspan 7, 12
World Wildlife Fund 20

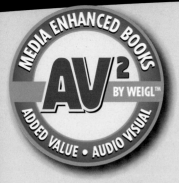

Log on to www.av2books.com

AV² by Weigl brings you media enhanced books that support active learning. Go to www.av2books.com, and enter the special code found on page 2 of this book. You will gain access to enriched and enhanced content that supplements and complements this book. Content includes video, audio, weblinks, quizzes, a slide show, and activities.

AV² Online Navigation

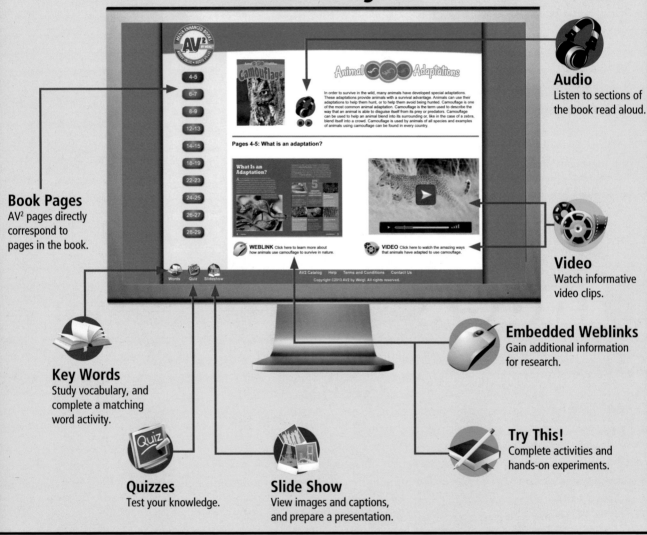

Audio
Listen to sections of the book read aloud.

Book Pages
AV² pages directly correspond to pages in the book.

Video
Watch informative video clips.

Embedded Weblinks
Gain additional information for research.

Key Words
Study vocabulary, and complete a matching word activity.

Try This!
Complete activities and hands-on experiments.

Quizzes
Test your knowledge.

Slide Show
View images and captions, and prepare a presentation.

AV² was built to bridge the gap between print and digital. We encourage you to tell us what you like and what you want to see in the future.

Sign up to be an AV² Ambassador at www.av2books.com/ambassador.